# ANNIE OAKLEY

# ANNIE OAKLEY

Published by Creative Education, 123 South Broad Street, Mankato, Minnesota 56001
Creative Education is an imprint of The Creative Company
Design and Production by EvansDay Design

Photographs by Buffalo Bill Historical Center; Cody Wyoming (*P.69.1193*, cover; p. 2; *P.69.1166*, p. 9;
Vincent Mercaldo Collection, *P.71.368.3*, p. 10; Gift of Dorothy Stone Collins in memory of her father,
Fred Stone, actor and friend of Annie Oakley and Frank Butler, *P.69.69*, p. 12; Vincent Mercaldo
Collection, *P.71.2722.1*, p. 15; Gift of the Coe Foundation, *1.69.73*, p. 33), Corbis (Bettmann, Paul
Edmondson, George H. H. Huey, Johan Springer Collection, Galen Rowell, Craig Tuttle, Ron Watts),
The Granger Collection, New York

Library of Congress Cataloging-in-Publication Data
Gilbert, Sara. Annie Oakley / by Sara Gilbert.
p. cm. — (Legends of the West)
Includes bibliographical references and index.
ISBN 1-58341-334-0

1. Oakley, Annie, 1860-1926—Juvenile literature. 2. Shooters of firearms—
United States—Biography—Juvenile literature. 3. Entertainers—United
States—Biography—Juvenile literature. 4. Women entertainers—United States—
Biography—Juvenile literature. I. Title. II. Legends of the West (Mankato, Minn.)
GV1157.O3G515 2005          799.3′092—dc22          2004058226 [B]

First edition

2 4 6 8 9 7 5 3 1

*Cover and page 2 photograph: Annie Oakley as a young woman*

## ⊷⊶ Sara Gilbert ⊷⊶

# ANNIE OAKLEY WAS A TINY WOMAN. AS AN ADULT, SHE WAS BARELY FIVE FEET (1.5 M) TALL AND WEIGHED NOT MUCH MORE THAN 100 POUNDS (45 KG). BUT SHE LIVED A LIFE THAT WAS BIG IN EVERY OTHER WAY.

Before she turned 10, Annie had become remarkably skilled with a rifle, which she used to help feed her poverty-stricken family and to pay off their debts. By the time she was 15, she was competing in shooting matches against men twice her age and winning easily.

# At 25, she was performing

## with one of the most famous Wild West

shows ever assembled. And when she died at the age of 66, she was known across the country and around the world as one of the best sharpshooters of all time, male or female.

Annie Oakley's legend has, of course, grown bigger as the years have passed. But even without exaggeration, most of what this tiny woman accomplished in her lifetime is truly amazing. With hard work and dedication to her craft, she rose out of poverty and into stardom. Along the way, she inspired countless young women to follow their dreams as well. Her larger-than-life legend continues to do that today.

# CHAPTER ONE

Happy Hunter

# PHOEBE ANN MOSES WAS BORN ON
# AUGUST 13, 1860,
## IN HER FAMILY'S HUMBLE HOME
# in Darke County, Ohio.

Although Jacob and Susan Moses were struggling farmers who already had four hungry children to feed, their new, dark-haired daughter was a welcome addition to the family.

Much was expected from Annie, as Phoebe preferred to be called, early on. The Moses children were responsible for many of the chores on the family farm and were often too busy to go to school. Annie and her sisters cleaned and cooked while the boys trapped small animals for food. Little Annie, who never liked domestic tasks, preferred to be outdoors hunting with her brothers.

When Annie was six years old, her father was stranded during a terrible snowstorm and died of pneumonia. His death left the already-poor Moses family in dire financial circumstances. Annie's mother, unable to properly feed and clothe all of the children on her own, eventually decided to send Annie away for awhile. At the age of eight, Annie was sent to live with a family friend who ran the Darke County Infirmary, an institution set up to take care of the elderly and the mentally ill as well as orphans. Annie helped take care of the other children there in exchange for housing, food, and an education.

One day, a man came to the infirmary looking for household help. When Annie heard about the request, she quickly volunteered her services. She wanted to earn whatever money she could to help her mother and siblings back home. Once she was able to convince the man that she could work hard despite being so petite, she was hired for a small wage.

But the job turned out to be nothing like she had expected. The family demanded that she work from morning to night, doing hard manual labor. She tended the farm animals, cooked the meals, fed the children, and cleaned the house. She didn't have time to rest, much less go to school as the man had promised. She felt like a servant. In her autobiography, Annie remembered suffering both physical and mental abuse while with the family. After enduring it for as long as possible, she ran away and returned to the infirmary.

*Neither her small stature, humble roots, nor abusive childhood could douse the determination that propelled Annie Oakley to fame.*

## Frank Butler

Frank Butler had a reputation as a skilled sharpshooter and vaudeville performer who traveled from town to town with a group of shooters, challenging local marksmen to a competition. That is exactly what he was doing when he met Annie Moses in Cincinnati in 1875. Before they met, Butler was quite boisterous about his own skill. He loudly claimed that he could outshoot "anything then living." He was humbled quite quickly, however, when a 15-year-old girl (Annie) outshot him. After marrying Annie and recognizing her great talent, Butler graciously gave the spotlight to her. His later life was devoted completely to his wife. After the pair retired in 1901, Butler became a representative for the Union Metallic Cartridge Company in Connecticut, which allowed both Annie and him to make endorsements for the company and to continue their shooting exhibitions. Butler also ran a gun club in North Carolina where Annie gave lessons and exhibitions.

Annie stayed at the infirmary for several more years and learned much from her caregivers. She learned to sew and was taught the basics of reading and writing. When she was about 13, she decided to return to her family and help them as much as she could.

While Annie had been away, her mother had remarried and had another child, only to be widowed a second time. Now Susan Moses was on her third husband—and still living in poverty. Her new husband, Joseph Shaw, was already well into middle age and unable to work hard to support the family. Annie decided to take matters into her own hands.

She found her father's old Kentucky rifle and started hunting small game such as quail, grouse, and rabbits. At first she used her catches to help feed her now six siblings. Then she sold the game to a grocery store in nearby Greenville. As her skill with a rifle became more well known, her birds quickly became a favorite at upscale hotels and restaurants 80 miles (129 km) away in Cincinnati.

Annie's birds and animals were favored by such businesses because they were always head-shot, which meant they were shot through the head. The rest of the meat was clean, not scattered with shotgun pellets or torn with a bullet. Restaurateurs liked to serve meals made of meat provided by Annie because they didn't have to worry about their customers breaking their teeth on pellets or picking shot out as they ate.

Annie's reputation as a skilled hunter earned her top dollar from her customers. Before long, the 15-year-old had made enough money to pay off the mortgage on her mother's house, as well as

This photo suggests the steady hands and cool confidence that earned Annie renown as a shooter when barely into her teens.

all of her family's other debts. This was a crowning achievement for Annie, who so badly wanted to ease her mother's burden. "Oh, how my heart leaped with joy as I handed the money to Mother and told her that I had saved enough to pay [the mortgage] off," she wrote in her autobiography.

Along with the money she earned came a certain prestige. Shooting contests became quite popular as the Civil War ended, and Annie enjoyed entering them. But she always competed against men. And most men didn't like to lose to a woman, much less a girl. Then Jack Frost, a hotel owner in Cincinnati who was one of Annie's regular customers, invited her to participate in a shooting contest against Frank E. Butler.

Butler was a well-known marksman who was touring the country and challenging local shooters to square off against him. He was surprised when he reached Cincinnati in 1875 and found that his competition would be a 15-year-old girl. "I almost dropped dead when a little slim girl in short dresses stepped out to the mark with me," Butler said later. "I was a beaten man the moment she appeared, for I was taken off guard."

Annie had to put up a $50 entry fee to shoot against Butler—a huge sum in those days (today, that would be equivalent to more than $500). But if she won, she stood to earn at least that much, perhaps even double. So, with the help of her brother, she found the money and entered the competition.

The shooting match was set up so that both competitors would have the chance to hit 25 targets. Whoever shot the most would win. Butler missed only one, but Annie got them all.

Butler lost more than a match and a handsome sum of money that day. He also lost his heart. The well-traveled sharpshooter fell in love with Annie and immediately began to court her. The following year, on August 23, 1876, the two were married. Annie was 16; her husband was 26.

For the first few years of their marriage, Frank remained the star of the traveling shooting troupe, which included several renowned marksmen who went from town to town putting on exhibitions. Annie stayed mostly in the shadows. But then, on May 1, 1882, Frank's regular partner became ill, and Annie had to step in. She held items for Frank to shoot at and did some shooting of her own as well. It was at about this time that Annie took her now-familiar stage name. Although she was always known in private as Mrs. Frank Butler, the world soon came to know her as the incredible Annie Oakley.

## *Taking Oakley as Her Name*

**A**nnie Oakley was given the name "Phoebe Ann Moses" at birth. Early on, she made it clear that she preferred to be called "Annie." But it was only once she took to the stage with her husband, Frank Butler, that she adopted her now-familiar last name, "Oakley." How she choose "Oakley," however, is the stuff of legend. One story suggests that it was the name of a town that Annie and Frank were passing through. Another similar story says that it was the name of a wooded suburb of Cincinnati that Annie found particularly attractive. Many others say it is the product of a joint brainstorm between Frank and Annie. However the name came to be, it stuck. Although Annie considered herself to be "Mrs. Frank Butler" and used that name offstage, she will always be known around the world for the name she gave herself: "Annie Oakley."

# CHAPTER TWO

# ❧Let the Show Begin☙

# ANNIE OAKLEY SOON

BECAME A REGULAR ONSTAGE WITH HER HUS-
BAND. TOGETHER, THEY TRAVELED ACROSS THE
COUNTRY, HELPING EACH OTHER WITH ACTS AND
PERFORMING THEIR OWN SIGNATURE TRICKS.

## One of their favorites included **their beloved poodle, George.**

The little white dog would sit on a stool with an apple bal-

anced on its head. Annie and Frank then took turns split-

ting the apple with a bullet, delighting the crowd each time.

One of those shows took place in St. Paul, Minnesota, in 1884. Among the people who had come to see Annie and Frank shoot was Chief Sitting Bull, the Lakota leader who had helped defeat General George Armstrong Custer at the Battle of the Little Bighorn eight years earlier. Annie thoroughly impressed Sitting Bull, who appreciated both her skill with a rifle and the way she carried herself in such a modest yet self-assured manner. She was in all ways a "proper lady."

Legend has it that Sitting Bull immediately arranged to meet Annie. The two became fast friends. Sitting Bull even asked the talented young woman if he could adopt her, perhaps seeking to replace his own daughter who had died after the Battle of the Little Bighorn. Annie agreed. The Lakota chief dubbed her *Watanya Cicilia*, which means "Little Sure Shot." That name followed her throughout her career.

The Butlers performed mostly in variety theaters and at skating rinks. Although they were popular, the couple made little money. "We were poor when we started," Annie remembered in her autobiography. "I remember my husband saying to me, 'Well, Annie, we have enough this week to buy you a pretty hat.'"

Later in 1884, Annie and Frank joined the Sells Brothers Circus as "champion rifle shots." The couple, however, was disappointed by the working conditions in the circus and left after only one season. Again, they struck out on their own, performing together for crowds wherever they went. But in 1885, everything changed.

Two years earlier, Colonel William F. Cody, better known as "Buffalo Bill," had put together a troupe of performers and started *Buffalo Bill's Wild West and Congress of Rough Riders of the World* show. The trav-

**SELLS BROTHERS'** ENORMOUS **UNITED** **SHOWS.**

MAGNIFICENT THREE RING CIRCUS,
FIVE CONTINENT MENAGERIE, HUGE ELEVATED STAGES,
AUSTRALIAN AVIARY,    AFRICAN AQUARIUM,
ROMAN HIPPODROME,
SPECTACULAR PAGEANTS, ARABIAN CARAVAN AND
TRANS-PACIFIC WILD BEAST EXHIBIT.

*The Sells Brothers Circus, of which Annie was a part for a short time, was a colorful mix of trick riders, acrobats, and exotic animals.*

## Thomas Edison

**T**homas Alva Edison is said to have had only three months of formal education. But with that, he became one of the greatest inventors in world history, compiling a total of 1,093 U.S. patents—the most issued to any individual. Perhaps Edison's most important inventions were those that gave the world electricity. He invented the first successful light bulb in 1879 (when Annie was 19 years old), set up the first electrical power distribution center, and created hundreds of other elements to make widespread electrical power possible. He also invented the phonograph and the movie camera and made significant improvements to the telegraph, the telephone, and motion picture technology in general. Edison devoted his life to inventing useful products that would serve society well, but he also created companies around the world that could manufacture and sell his many inventions. He is well-known for his commitment to hard work and was fond of saying, "Genius is 1 percent inspiration and 99 percent perspiration."

eling production was designed to spotlight the talents of Buffalo Bill and his crew of cowboys, scouts, and Indians. The show included riding stunts, a mock bison hunt, battle and stagecoach robbery reenactments, and, of course, sharpshooting acts. The Butlers had tried to join the group when it started in 1883, but they were turned down because the show already had a full staff of shooters. When the lead marksman left the show in 1885, the door was wide open for Frank and Annie.

Some say that Buffalo Bill was reluctant to bring a woman sharpshooter into his cast and that he took Annie only on a trial basis. But it didn't take long for him to realize that she was a great asset to his show. He was charmed by her talent and poise and took to calling her "Missie." Soon, Annie's name and face were plastered on the show's advertising posters with the words "Champion Markswoman" underneath them.

Suddenly, Annie was in the limelight. Her husband, who for years had been the star of the show, graciously stepped back and let her enjoy success. He was delighted for his wife and was more than happy to serve as her manager and assistant. He devoted himself to promoting her and building her career.

With Buffalo Bill's show as her backdrop and Frank Butler as her assistant, Annie Oakley became increasingly popular. She earned the second spot in Buffalo Bill's program, just after the show's namesake himself. Buffalo Bill said he brought her out early to put the women in the audience at ease and to show them that not all shooting was harmful. But besides that, the crowd was clamoring for her. She was easily the biggest draw of the show.

One of Annie's most famous trick shots involved shooting backwards over her shoulder using just a hand mirror for aim.

Annie would shoot glass balls, clay pigeons, and even dimes thrown into the air. She could "scramble" eggs in midair and hit targets behind her using a mirror. One of her best-known tricks involved splitting playing cards held with the thin edge facing her and then puncturing them five or six times as they fell to the ground. Cards with holes shot through them were often given as complimentary tickets and became known as "Annie Oakleys," a name that is still often used to refer to free tickets today.

In 1887, Buffalo Bill took his show to Europe. The troupe toured England and joined in the Golden Jubilee of Queen Victoria's reign as queen of the British Empire. Annie was the biggest news of the event. Her childlike charm (she was known for giving a girlish skip after performing her acts) and her incredible skill earned her hordes of fans in England, including the queen herself. It is said that Queen Victoria presented Annie with a beautiful silver dish to thank her for her performance.

Europeans were infatuated with the image of the American West. They loved the costumes the performers wore, including Annie's buckskin jackets and fringed skirts. They loved the wild portrayals of cowboys and Indians. And so Buffalo Bill's show was welcomed back to Europe for a second tour in 1889, when it spent time in France, Italy, Spain, and Germany. During a performance in Germany, Annie successfully shot the ashes off a cigarette held in the lips of the crown prince of Germany, at his request. That crown prince later became Kaiser Wilhelm II.

Annie and Frank went wherever the show went, including to Chicago, Illinois, for the World's Columbian Exposition in 1893 and to North Platte, Nebraska, in 1896. Annie was 36 years old when she took her first trip to the West (she'd never been farther west than her Ohio home), despite already having a reputation around the world as a true Western legend.

In 1894, inventor Thomas Edison recruited Annie to do a shooting demonstration for him to film with his newly invented movie camera. He had already filmed Buffalo Bill and other members of the cast, but he especially wanted Annie so he could study how his cameras followed the flight of a speeding bullet. Edison made the films of Annie and the cast into nickelodeons—films that were shown for a five-cent ticket price.

Tragically, in 1901, a train carrying Buffalo Bill's troupe collided with another train as it sped through North Carolina. More than 100 horses were killed in the accident, and dozens of people were injured—including Annie, who had to have several operations to repair her injured back. Many people wondered if the shooting star would ever return to show business.

Indeed, Annie and Frank decided to retire from *Buffalo Bill's Wild West* that year. The injury was only part of the reason. The couple had grown weary of travel and wanted to spend more time at the home they had purchased in New Jersey years earlier. They settled down for a more domestic life. But it would be hard for them to stay that way.

## Saddle Up

Annie Oakley was not a Western girl. She grew up in Ohio and was in her 30s before she even went west. And, contrary to some reports, she was not an expert horsewoman at an early age. Some stories say that Annie learned to ride a horse as a young girl. Some say the farmer who hired her as household help taught her. But the truth seems to be that she didn't learn to ride until she and her husband, Frank, joined *Buffalo Bill's Wild West*. In fact, some say that Buffalo Bill Cody himself taught young Annie to ride a horse and twirl a lasso. The first recorded mention of Annie riding a horse came in 1886, a year after she and Frank joined the cast of the *Wild West*. Annie rode into the ring and shot from horseback. Over the following years, she performed many of her tricks from the saddle. Some depictions even show her standing on a galloping horse while shooting at targets.

# CHAPTER THREE

# Back in Business

HOUSEKEEPING HAD NEVER BEEN ANNIE OAKLEY'S FAVORITE CHORE. SHE WAS REMINDED OF THIS

# AT THE AGE OF 41,

## when she found herself retired and in a home of her own for the first time since childhood.

And although she herself was not a good housekeeper, she also did not enjoy having servants take care of her domestic affairs. Three years after retiring from show business, Annie and Frank sold their house in New Jersey and took to the road again.

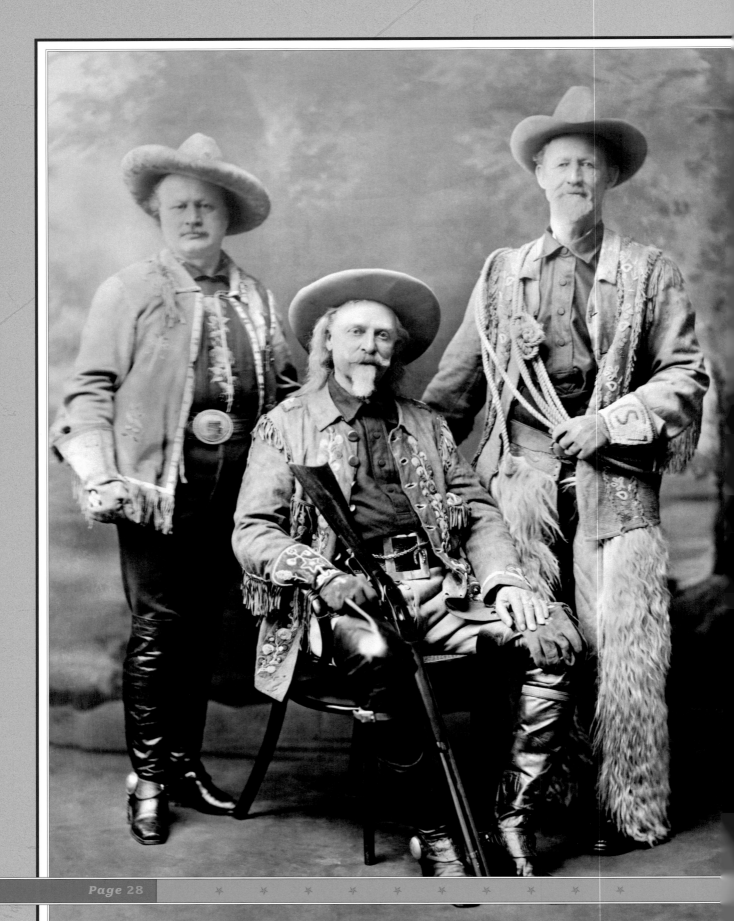

Buffalo Bill's Wild West, *starring Buffalo Bill Cody (center), became known far and wide in the late 1800s and early 1900s.*

The couple did not return to *Buffalo Bill's Wild West*, however, choosing instead to perform on their own and in various other shooting arenas. They participated in exhibitions for the Union Metallic Cartridge Company and the Remington Arms Company. They also took part in public shooting matches. In 1911, they joined another show, *The Young Buffalo Show*, and traveled with it for two years. But in 1913, Annie and Frank again decided to retire and settle down.

The couple built a house in Cambridge, Maryland, where they spent their days hunting, fishing, and entertaining friends. Annie also started writing stories about her life, many of which were published in sportsmen's magazines. She penned a short shooting autobiography that was published in 1914 by the DuPont Powder Company, an ammunition manufacturer. In it, she listed all of the different gunpowders she had used in her many shooting exhibitions and told of the difficulty she had had smuggling her favorite powders into European countries. One story involved her first trip to France, where no foreign powders were allowed. Annie wrote that she filled a rubber hot-water bottle with her powder and put it under the bustle of her dress. "Bustles were quite the rage in those days," she wrote, "and although I had never worn them, I was glad to on this occasion."

But again, adventurous Annie grew bored with her domestic duties. Although she had enjoyed offering her opinions on the design of the house—notably, requesting that the sink and work areas in the kitchen be suitable for a woman of her small stature—she did

## Sitting Bull

Chief Sitting Bull was born in what is now South Dakota and was given the name *Hunkesni*, which means "slow." After he showed great bravery in a battle during his adolescence, his father changed his name to *Tatanka-Iyotanka*, which describes a bull that is sitting on its haunches and is immovable. Sitting Bull is best-known as a Lakota medicine man who took part in the Battle of the Little Bighorn, which is also known as Custer's Last Stand. He was among the 1,000 warriors who killed General George Armstrong Custer and his entire troop of 210 soldiers on June 25, 1876. Sitting Bull and his followers were driven into Canada after that battle but returned after accepting a promise of amnesty (a pardon) from the U.S. government in 1881. Sitting Bull spent two years confined at Fort Randall in South Dakota. In 1885, he joined *Buffalo Bill's Wild West*. Sitting Bull was killed in a conflict with Indian policemen in 1890.

not enjoy taking care of the home. "I went all to pieces under the care of a house," she admitted at the time. Her husband agreed. He was once quoted as saying, "She was a rotten housekeeper. Her record in this department was seven cooks in five days."

By the time a year of retirement had passed, Annie was restless. Her husband noticed her unhappiness and decided to take her on a road trip across the country. They traveled south, where they became enchanted with the small resort town of Pinehurst, North Carolina.

In Pinehurst, the Butlers found an active social life as well as the opportunity to give shooting exhibitions and to offer shooting lessons to resort guests. Annie particularly enjoyed teaching women the art of shooting; hundreds of women learned from her over the years. When the U.S. joined World War I in 1917, Annie even offered to train a regiment of women volunteers to help the cause. Her offer was never accepted.

In 1917, Annie and Frank learned that Buffalo Bill Cody, their longtime friend and employer, had died. He had sold his show in 1913 but had continued performing in other productions. His death marked the end of an era for Annie and Frank as well as for the country. Annie wrote a long eulogy for Buffalo Bill, mourning both his passing and the passing of the golden Wild West era.

But even if that era was over, Annie Oakley's career was not. As she approached her 60th birthday, she continued to perform with her husband and their new dog, Dave. And her shows now also had another dimension. She took time to remind her fans how hard she had fought for her right to compete against men and to perform in male-dominated shows. She also pointed out that she had always been a lady and that she had taken great pains to act and dress properly despite her profession. It was clear that she and Frank, who had both always dressed modestly and acted with great decorum, did not approve of the revealing costumes and boisterous actions of some of the other performers of the time.

Over the years, the Butlers had been able to make and save large sums of money. They were very careful with their money, but they were also very generous. Much of their income went to Annie's family in Ohio, especially her mother and her many nieces and nephews. But the couple, who never had children of their own, also supported at least a dozen orphans and others they met during their travels. During World War I, Annie and Frank helped raise money for the Red Cross and traveled across the country giving shooting demonstrations at training camps.

In 1922, at the age of 62, Annie mounted another comeback. She scheduled performances in several major cities along the East Coast, including New York City and her beloved Pinehurst. In Brockton, Massachusetts, 100,000 people showed up for her exhibition, and Annie did not let them down. She was still able to hit a remarkable number of targets and perform many of her trademark tricks. In Pinehurst, she hit 100 clay targets from the 16-yard (14.6 m) mark.

But at the end of that year, Annie and Frank were severely injured in an automobile accident. The accident stalled Annie's

# BUFFALO BILL'S WILD WEST·
## CONGRESS, ROUGH RIDERS OF THE WORLD.

A. Hoen & Co., Baltimore, U.S.A

# MISS ANNIE OAKLEY,
## THE PEERLESS LADY WING-SHOT.

*Annie became a huge attraction for Buffalo Bill's Wild West and remained a beloved star for more than 40 years.*

comeback and derailed plans she had made to star in a movie. It took more than a year for her to recover from her injuries, but she was again performing on the show circuit and setting new shooting records by 1924.

Sadly, that comeback would be Annie's last hurrah. By 1925, she was beginning to slow down. Now in her mid-60s, she was frail, and her health was failing. She and Frank moved back to Ohio where they could be closer to her family. Although the couple attended local shooting matches, they were no longer able to participate. Annie spent her quiet time writing her memoirs, which were published in newspapers around the country.

On August 23, 1926, the Butlers celebrated their 50th wedding anniversary. Just a few months later, on November 3, Annie Oakley died of natural causes. Frank Butler died just three weeks later, on November 21. They were buried side-by-side in Greenville, Ohio, on Thanksgiving Day.

## Going Gray

It is true that Annie Oakley and her husband were onboard a train that crashed in 1901 and that Annie was one of hundreds of people severely injured in the accident. What is most likely not true, however, is the legend that her always-long and always-dark hair turned white immediately afterward. At the time of the accident, Annie was 41 years old. More than likely, her brown hair was flecked with gray by then. But there is no evidence that she suddenly went white after the accident. In fact, photos taken well after the accident show Annie with a full head of dark hair. The train accident did temporarily paralyze her, however, and she had at least five surgeries to correct the damage to her spine. But the accident did not cause her to go gray, nor did it stop the tireless performer from going on with the show.

LEGEND VERSUS FACT

# CHAPTER FOUR

# Still a Shooting Star

AT THE TIME OF HER DEATH,

# ANNIE OAKLEY'S

NAME AND ABILITIES WERE KNOWN AROUND THE WORLD. HER 17 YEARS IN

## *Buffalo Bill's Wild West,*

as well as all of her personal accomplishments,

had made her a household name.

She may have been the most famous woman in the country, if not the world, at the time. But, as so often happens, the legend of Annie Oakley grew larger after she died.

*Betty Hutton glamorized the role of Annie Oakley in a 1950 movie production of Annie Get Your Gun.*

The first retelling of her life came in 1935, in a movie starring Barbara Stanwyck as Annie. Then, in 1946, two decades after Annie's death, the story of her life was retold in the lively Broadway musical *Annie Get Your Gun*. Although the production, written by Herbert and Dorothy Fields and produced by Richard Rodgers and Oscar Hammerstein II, embellished many of the details of her life and took much theatrical liberty with the story, it has become one of the most lasting reminders of Annie Oakley.

*Annie Get Your Gun* premiered at the Imperial Theatre in New York on May 16, 1946. With Ethel Merman in the title role and 10 songs by renowned composer Irving Berlin, including "There's No Business Like Show Business," "Doin' What Comes Natur'lly," and "Anything You Can Do," the show became an instant hit. It played on Broadway for 1,147 performances, making it the third-longest-running musical of the 1940s.

It didn't take long for Hollywood to notice the popularity of the musical. In 1950, MGM produced *Annie Get Your Gun* for the big screen. Comedienne Betty Hutton played Annie, and Howard Keel played Frank Butler. At $3 million, it was the most expensive musical MGM had made to date, but it went on to become one of the studio's highest-grossing films of all time and won an Oscar for best motion picture score. In 2000, the studio released a 50th anniversary edition of the film on video and DVD, the first time it had ever been available on home video.

## Buffalo Bill

Few people are as closely associated with the legend of the West as William F. Cody, better known as "Buffalo Bill." By the time Cody started *Buffalo Bill's Wild West* in 1883, he had already experienced a colorful career as a Pony Express rider, a Union scout during the Civil War, and a buffalo hunter who claimed to have killed 4,280 buffalo in 17 months. He had even tried his hand at show business, acting in several Western plays in the 1870s. But Cody's crowning achievement, and that for which he is most remembered, was organizing the traveling show that bore his name. *Buffalo Bill's Wild West*, with its wild reenactments of all things Western, remained popular until Cody sold it in 1913. He died four years later, on January 10, 1917, and is buried at the summit of Lookout Mountain near Denver, Colorado.

Shortly after the original film was released, a short-lived television program loosely based on Annie Oakley's life also became popular. Originally known as *Annie Oakley and Tagg* before the title was shortened to just *Annie Oakley*, the show starred Gail Davis as Annie and ran from 1952 until 1956.

In 1999, a revival of *Annie Get Your Gun* opened on Broadway featuring Bernadette Peters; later, soap opera star Susan Lucci also played Annie. In the name of political correctness, the modern version featured a few changes—most notably, the absence of the Irving Berlin song "I'm an Indian Too."

Stage and film adaptations of her life only fueled public interest in the real story of Annie Oakley. That interest lingers almost a century after her death. Much has been written about her, from fanciful children's stories and fictional novels to factual biographies. Photographs of her life have been collected in books, and reproductions of posters from her days with *Buffalo Bill's Wild West* have been made available. Many collectibles, from figurines of Annie or her horse to replications of her clothing and hats, are bought and sold on auction sites such as eBay. To this day, Annie Oakley memorabilia and artifacts are prized possessions in Western collectors' markets.

Many of Annie's surviving guns, medals, and trophies are now housed in museums around the country. The Garst Museum, located near her birthplace in Greenville, Ohio, has the largest known

*In 1922, at 62 years of age, Annie was still quite active. She is pictured here teaching a young woman how to shoot.*

collection of Annie Oakley artifacts in the world, many of which were given to the museum by her relatives in the area. The Annie Oakley room contains guns, clothing, dishes, glassware, and gifts that had been given to the sharpshooter by her adoring fans. One of the trunks she used during her travels is on display as well.

The Buffalo Bill Historical Center in Cody, Wyoming, also has an extensive collection that incorporates much of Annie's career with *Buffalo Bill's Wild West*. Original show posters, souvenirs from the show, and many photographs help bring to life both the show and Annie Oakley's role in it. Other museums, including the National Women's Hall of Fame in Seneca Falls, New York, pay tribute to Annie's life and her impact on society today.

For the past four decades, Annie has also been honored with the Annie Oakley Days Festival, held at the Darke County Fairgrounds in Greenville, Ohio. The weekend event, which includes a parade, shooting contests, and the crowning of "Miss Annie Oakley," celebrates the legacy of one of Ohio's most famous residents.

In 1995, the house that Annie and Frank built as a retirement home in Cambridge, Maryland, was placed on the National Register of Historic Places. It is the only surviving residence that Annie Oakley either owned or occupied.

Even though many decades have passed since her death, Annie Oakley's story still shines as brightly as it did in the early 1900s. From the continuing stage productions of *Annie Get Your*

*Gun*, which has been performed in community theaters and high school auditoriums as well as major venues around the world, to the dozens of books and films now available about her life, her legend grows stronger with time. And although there are few opportunities to compete in shooting matches today, Annie Oakley is still regarded as a hero to many young girls and women. Annie believed that women could do anything they set their minds to, especially if men told them they couldn't. She was a champion for women's rights long before it became popular to be one.

Of course, Annie Oakley didn't set out to change the world when she embarked on her legendary career as a sharpshooter. She was just doing what she did best. Along the way, she found great fame and prosperity. She also became a role model for many, many women. And that may be the most lasting part of her legacy.

## *Melting Her Medals*

Annie Oakley gave much of what she made as a shooting star to her mother and various charities, including orphanages and individual orphans. Much of her generosity is a matter of record. But there is one legend about her giving that may or may not be true. It is said that near the end of her life, Annie took the hundreds of gold medals she had earned in shooting competitions and had them all melted down and made into solid gold bricks. The story suggests that she sold the gold and gave the money to a children's home somewhere in the South. Annie, who did indeed win numerous medals throughout her years of competing, may well have done this generous act. But not all sources agree that it actually happened. There is no question, however, that she was very generous with the money she earned.

# Further Information

**BOOKS**

Flynn, Jean. *Annie Oakley, Legendary Sharpshooter*. Berkeley Heights, N.J.: Enslow Publishers, 1998.

Kasper, Shirl. *Annie Oakley*. Norman, Okla.: University of Oklahoma Press, 2000.

Riley, Glenda. *The Life and Legacy of Annie Oakley*. Norman, Okla.: University of Oklahoma Press, 2002.

**FILMS**

*American Tall Tales and Legends: Annie Oakley*. 1998. 50 min. Lyrick Studios.

*Annie Get Your Gun*. 1950. 121 min. Warner Home Video.

*Annie Oakley*. 1935. 90 min. Turner Home Entertainment.

**WEB SITES**

American Cowboys: Women of the West
http://www.thewildwest.org/cowboys/women/oakley.html

Buffalo Bill Historical Center
http://www.bbhc.org/bbm/biographyAO.cfm

National Women's Hall of Fame
http://www.greatwomen.org/women.php?action=viewone&id=114

# Index